Hippocrene

CHILDREN'S ILLUSTRATED FRENCH DICTIONARY

ENGLISH · FRENCH
FRENCH · ENGLISH

W9-CFG-924

Compiled and translated by the Editors of Hippocrene Books

Interior illustrations by S. Grant (24, 81, 88); J. Gress (page 10, 21, 24, 37, 46, 54, 59, 65, 72, 75, 77);
K. Migliorelli (page 13, 14, 18, 19, 20, 21, 22, 25, 31, 32, 37, 39, 40, 46, 47, 66, 71, 75, 76, 82, 86, 87);
B. Swidzinska (page 9, 11, 12, 13, 14, 16, 23, 27, 28, 30, 32, 33, 35, 37, 38, 41, 42, 45, 46, 47, 48, 49, 50, 52,
53, 56, 57, 58, 59, 60, 61, 62, 63, 66, 68, 69, 70, 71, 72, 73, 75, 77, 78, 79, 83), N. Zhukov (page 8, 13, 14,
17, 18, 23, 27, 29, 33, 34, 39, 40, 41, 52, 64, 65, 71, 72, 73, 78, 84, 86, 88).

Design, prepress, and production: Graafiset International, Inc.

Copyright © 1999 by Hippocrene Books, Inc.

All rights reserved.

Cataloging-in-Publication Data available from the Library of Congress.

ISBN 0-7818-0710-7 (Hardcover edition, 1999)
ISBN 0-7818-0847-2 (Paperback edition, 2001)

Printed in Hong Kong

For information, address:
Hippocrene Books, Inc.
171 Madison Avenue
New York, NY 10016

INTRODUCTION

With their absorbent minds, infinite curiosities and excellent memories, children have enormous capacities to master many languages. All they need is exposure and encouragement.

The easiest way to learn a foreign language is to simulate the same natural method by which a child learns English. The natural technique is built on the concept that language is representational of concrete objects and ideas. The use of pictures and words are the natural way for children to begin to acquire a new language.

The concept of this Illustrated Dictionary is to allow children to build vocabulary and initial competency naturally. Looking at the pictorial content of the Dictionary and saying and matching the words in connection to the drawings gives children the opportunity to discover the foreign language and thus, a new way to communicate.

The drawings in the Dictionary are designed to capture children's imaginations and make the learning process interesting and entertaining, as children return to a word and picture repeatedly until they begin to recognize it.

The beautiful images and clear presentation make this dictionary a wonderful tool for unlocking your child's multilingual potential.

Deborah Dumont, M.A., M.Ed.,
Child Psychologist and Educational Consultant

French Pronunciation

Letter	Pronunciation system used
a	**ah** like the *a* in English 'art'
ai	**ay** as in English 'hay'
am, an	**on** a dull *o* followed by a nasal *n*
au	**oh** like the *o* in English 'omit'
b	**b** as in English 'bent'
c, ç	**s** like the hissing *s* in English 'beside'
c	**k** like *c* in English 'cat'
d	**d** as in English 'day'
e	**uh** a short dull, almost mute *e*
é	**eh** like in English 'café'
eau	**oh** like the *o* in English 'omit'
en, em	**on** a dull *o* followed by a nasal *n*
eu	**oe** an uh-sound formed by pursing both lips
f	**f** as in English 'fire'
ge	**j** as in English 'jewel' with a heavy h-sound added
ga	**g** as in English 'garden'
h	a mute *h*
i	**ee** as in English 'see'
im, in	**an** a dull *a* followed by a nasal *n*
j	**j** as in English 'just' with a heavy h-sound added
k	**k** as in English 'key'
l	**l** as in English 'land'
m	**m** as in English 'man'
n	**n** as in English 'no'
o	**oh** like the *o* in English 'omit'
oi	**wah** like in English 'water'
ou	**oo** as in English 'room'
p	**p** as in English 'pet'
qu	**k** as in English 'key'
r	**r** an *r* formed by pressing the tongue to the lower palate
s	**s** like the hissing *s* in English 'beside'
t	**t** as in English 'today'
u	**u** an u-sound like *u* in 'cue'
v	**v** as in English 'vowel'
w	**w** as in English 'wet'
y	**y** like in English 'hymn'
z	**z** as in English 'zebra'

airplane   **l'avion**
(l)ah-vee-yohn

alligator   **l'alligator**
(l)ah-lee-gah-tohr

alphabet   **l'alphabet**
(l)ahl-fah-beh

antelope   **l'antilope**
(l)on-tee-lohp

antlers   **(les) bois**
(lay) bwah

apple　　**(la) pomme**
(lah) pohm

aquarium　　**l'aquarium**
(l)ah-quah-ree-yom

arch　　**(la) voûte**
(lah) voot

arrow　　**(la) flèche**
(lah) flesh

autumn　　**l'automne**
(l)oh-ton

baby   **(le) bébé**
(luh) beh-beh

backpack   **(le) sac à dos**
(luh) sahk ah doh

badger   **(le) blaireau**
(luh) blay-roh

baker   **(le) boulanger**
(luh) boo-lon-jay

ball   **(la) balle**
(lah) bahl

balloon   **(le) ballon**
(luh) bahl-lohn

banana   **(la) banane**
(lah) bah-nahn

barley   **l'orge**
(l)ohrj

barrel   **(le) tonneau**
(luh) toh-noh

basket   **(le) panier**
(luh) pahn-yay

bat   **(la) chauve-souris**
(lah) chohf-soo-ree

beach   **(la) plage**
(lah) plahj

bear　　　　　　　**l'ours**
(l)oors

beaver　　　　　　**(le) castor**
(luh) kahs-tohr

bed　　　　　　　**(le) lit**
(luh) lee

bee　　　　　　　**l'abeille**
(l)ah-bay

beetle　　　　　　**l'insecte**
(l)an-sehkt

bell　　　　　　　**(la) cloche**
(lah) clohsh

belt **(la) ceinture**
(lah) sayn-tur

bench **(le) banc**
(luh) bon

bicycle **(la) bicyclette**
(lah) bee-see-clet

binoculars **(les) jumelles**
(lay) ju-mel

bird **l'oiseau**
(l)wah-zoh

birdcage **(la) cage**
(lah) kahj

black **noir**
nwahr

blocks **(les) blocs**
(lay) blohk

blossom **(la) fleur**
(lah) floer

blue **bleu**
bloe

boat **(le) bateau**
(luh) bah-toh

bone **l'os**
(l)ohs

book   **(le) livre**
(luh) lee-vr

boot   **(la) botte**
(lah) boht

bottle   **(la) bouteille**
(lah) boo-tay

bowl   **(le) bol**
(luh) bohl

boy   **(le) garçon**
(luh) gahr-sohn

bracelet   **(le) bracelet**
(luh) brahs-leh

branch **(la) branche**
(lah) bronsh

bread **(le) pain**
(luh) payn

breakfast **(le) petit déjeuner**
(luh) puh-tee deh-joe-nay

bridge **(le) pont**
(luh) pohn

broom **(le) balai**
(luh) bah-lay

brother **(le) frère**
(luh) frayr

brown   **marron**
mah-rohn

brush   **(la) brosse**
(lah) brohs

bucket   **(le) seau**
(luh) soh

bulletin board (le) tableau d'affichage
(luh) tah-bloh dah-fee-shahj

bumblebee   **(le) bourdon**
(luh) boor-dohn

butterfly   **(le) papillon**
(luh) pah-pee-yohn

cab   **(le) taxi**
(luh) tahk-see

cabbage   **(le) chou**
(luh) shoo

cactus   **(le) cactus**
(luh) kahk-tus

café   **(le) café**
(luh) kah-feh

cake   **(le) gâteau**
(luh) gah-toh

camel   **(le) chameau**
(luh) shah-moh

camera   **l'appareil de photo**
(l)ah-pah-ray duh foh-toh

candle   **(la) bougie**
(lah) boo-jee

candy   **(le) bonbon**
(luh) bohn-bohn

canoe   **(le) canoë**
(luh) kah-noh-eh

cap   **(la) casquette**
(lah) kahs-ket

captain   **(le) capitaine**
(luh) kah-pee-tayn

car   **(la) voiture**
(lah) vwah-ture

card   **(la) carte**
(lah) kahrt

carpet   **(le) tapis**
(luh) tah-pee

carrot   **(la) carotte**
(lah) kah-roht

(to) carry   **porter**
pohr-tay

castle   **(le) château**
(luh) shah-toh

cat   **(le) chat**
(luh) shah

cave   **(la) grotte**
(lah) groht

chair   **(la) chaise**
(lah) shayz

cheese   **(le) fromage**
(luh) froh-mahj

cherry   **(la) cerise**
(lah) suh-reez

chimney   **(la) cheminée**
(lah) shuh-mee-neh

chocolate   **le chocolat**
(luh) shoh-koh-lah

Christmas tree   **l'arbre de Noël**
(l)ahr-br duh noh-el

circus   **(le) cirque**
(luh) seerk

(to) climb   **grimper**
gran-pay

cloud   **(le) nuage**
(luh) nu-wahj

clown   **(le) clown**
(luh) cloon

coach　　　**(le) carrosse**
(luh) kah-rohs

coat　　　**(le) manteau**
(luh) mon-toh

coconut　　　**(la) noix de coco**
(lah) nwah duh koh-koh

comb　　　**(le) peigne**
(luh) payn-ye

comforter　　　**(la) couette**
(lah) koo-et

compass　　　**(la) boussole**
(lah) boos-sohl

(to) cook　　　　**cuisiner**
kuee-zee-nay

cork　　　　**(le) liège**
(luh) lee-ayj

corn　　　　**(le) maïs**
(luh) mah-ees

cow　　　　**(la) vache**
(lah) vahsh

cracker　　　　**(le) biscuit**
(luh) bees-kuee

cradle　　　　**(le) berceau**
(luh) bayr-soh

(to) crawl **marcher à quatre pattes**
mahr-shay ah kah-tr paht

(to) cross **traverser**
trah-vayr-say

crown **(la) couronne**
(lah) koo-rohn

(to) cry **pleurer**
ploe-ray

cucumber **(le) concombre**
(luh) cohn-cohm-br

curtain **(le) rideau**
(luh) ree-doh

(to) dance   **danser**
don-say

dandelion

(le) pissenlit
(luh) pees-on-lee

date   **(la) date**
(lah) daht

deer

(la) biche
(lah) beesh

desert   **(le) désert**
(luh) deh-sayr

desk   **(le) bureau**
(luh) bu-roh

dirty   **sale**
sahl

dog **(le) chien**
(luh) shee-yon

doghouse **(la) niche**
(lah) neesh

doll **(la) poupée**
(lah) poo-peh

dollhouse **(la) maison de poupée**
(lah) may-zohn duh poo-peh

dolphin **(le) dauphin**
(luh) doh-fan

donkey **l'âne**
(l)ahn

dragon **(le) dragon**
(luh) drah-gohn

dragonfly   **(la) libellule**
(lah) lee-buh-lul

(to) draw   **dessiner**
duh-see-nay

dress   **(la) robe**
(lah) rohb

(to) drink   **boire**
bwahr

drum   **(le) tambour**
(luh) ton-boor

duck   **(le) canard**
(lah) kah-nahr

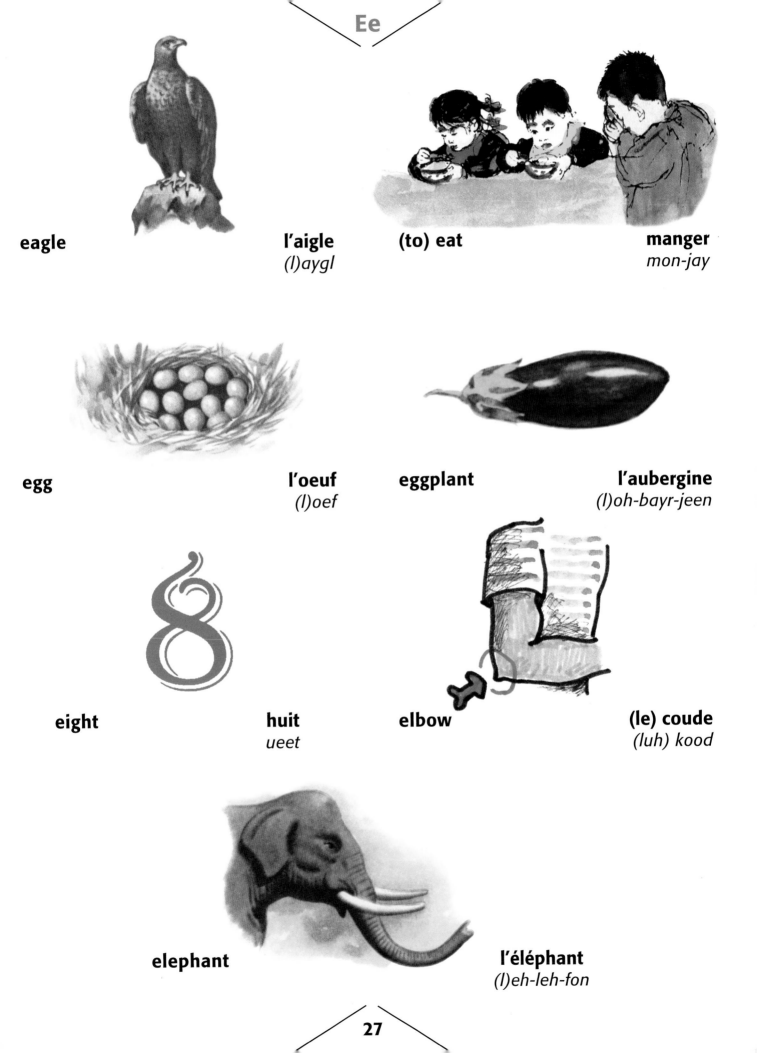

eagle   **l'aigle**
(l)aygl

(to) eat   **manger**
mon-jay

egg   **l'oeuf**
(l)oef

eggplant   **l'aubergine**
(l)oh-bayr-jeen

eight   **huit**
ueet

elbow   **(le) coude**
(luh) kood

elephant   **l'éléphant**
(l)eh-leh-fon

empty   **vide**
veed

engine   **(la) locomotive**
(lah) loh-koh-moh-teev

envelope   **l'enveloppe**
(l)on-vuh-lohp

escalator   **l'escalier roulant**
(l)ays-kahl-yay roo-lon

Eskimo   **l'esquimau**
(l)ays-kee-moh

(to) explore   **explorer**
ex-ploh-ray

eye   **l'oeil**
(l)oiy

face   **(le) visage**
(luh) vee-zahj

fan   **(le) ventilateur**
(luh) von-tee-lah-toer

father   **(le) père**
(luh) payr

fear   **(la) peur**
(lah) poer

feather   **(la) plume**
(lah) plume

(to) feed   **nourrir**
noo-reer

fence **(la) clôture**
(lah) kloh-ture

fern **(la) fougère**
(lah) foo-jayr

field **(le) champ**
(luh) shon

field mouse **(la) souris des champs**
(lah) soo-ree day shon

finger **(le) doigt**
(luh) dwah

fir tree **(le) sapin**
(luh) sah-pan

fire   **(le) feu**
(luh) foe

fish   **(le) poisson**
(luh) pwah-sohn

(to) fish   **pêcher**
pay-shay

fist   **(le) poing**
(luh) pwahn

five   **cinq**
sank

flag   **(le) drapeau**
(luh) drah-poh

flashlight　　**(la) torche électrique**
(lah) tohrsh eh-layk-treek

(to) float　　**flotter**
floh-tay

flower　　**(la) fleur**
(lah) floer

(to) fly　　**voler**
voh-lay

foot　　**(le) pied**
(luh) pee-yay

fork　　**(la) fourchette**
(lah) foor-shet

fountain　　**(la) fontaine**
(lah) fohn-tayn

four **quatre**
kah-tr

fox

(le) renard
(luh) ruh-nahr

frame **(le) cadre**
(luh) kah-dr

friend **l'ami**
(l)ah-mee

frog **(la) grenouille**
(lah) gruh-noo-ye

fruit **(le) fruit**
(luh) froo-ee

furniture **(le) meuble**
(luh) moe-bl

garden   **(le) jardin**
(luh) jahr-dan

gate   **(la) porte**
(lah) pohrt

(to) gather   **cueillir**
koiy-yeer

geranium   **(le) géranium**
(luh) jeh-rah-nee-yom

giraffe   **(la) girafe**
(lah) jee-rahf

girl   **(la) fille**
(lah) fee

(to) give **donner**
dohn-nay

glass **(le) verre**
(luh) vayr

glasses **(les) lunettes**
(lay) lu-net

globe **(le) globe**
(luh) glohb

glove **(le) gant**
(luh) gon

goat **(la) chèvre**
(lah) shay-vr

goldfish **(le) poisson rouge**
(luh) pwah-sohn rooj

"Good night" **"Bonne nuit"**
bohn noo-ee

"Good-bye" **"Au revoir"**
oh ruh-vwahr

goose **l'oie**
(l)wah

grandfather **(le) grand-père**
(luh) gron-payr

grandmother **(la) grand-mère**
(lah) gron-mayr

grapes　　　**(les) raisins**
(lay) ray-zan

grasshopper　　　**(la) sauterelle**
(lah) soh-tuh-rel

green　　　**vert**
vayr

greenhouse　　　**(la) serre**
(la) sayr

guitar　　　**(la) guitare**
(lah) gee-tahr

hammer　　　　**(le) marteau**
(luh) mahr-toh

hammock　　　　**(le) hamac**
(luh) ah-mak

hamster　　　　**(le) hamster**
(luh) ahm-stare

hand　　　　**(la) main**
(lah) mayn

handbag　　　　**(le) sac à main**
(luh) sahk ah-mayn

handkerchief　　　　**(le) mouchoir**
(luh) moo-shwahr

harvest **(la) moisson**
(lah) mwah-sohn

hat **(le) chapeau**
(luh) shah-poh

hay **(le) foin**
(luh) fwahn

headdress **(le) panache**
(luh) pah-nahsh

heart **(le) coeur**
(luh) koer

hedgehog **(le) hérisson**
(luh) eh-ree-sohn

hen   **(la) poule**
(lah) pool

(to) hide   **se cacher**
suh cah-shay

highway   **l'autoroute**
(l)oh-toh-root

honey   **(le) miel**
(luh) mee-ayl

horns   **(les) cornes**
(lay) kohrn

horse   **(le) cheval**
(luh) shuh-vahl

horseshoe **(le) fer à cheval**
(luh) fayr ah shuh-vahl

hourglass **(le) sablier**
(luh) sah-blee-yay

house **(la) maison**
(lah) may-zohn

(to) hug **embrasser**
om-brah-say

hydrant **(la) prise d'eau**
(lah) preez doh

ice cream **(la) glace**
(lah) glahs

ice cubes **(les) glaçons**
(lay) glahs-sohn

ice-skating **(le) patin à glace**
(luh) pah-tan ah-glahs

instrument **l'instrument**
(l)ans-tru-mon

iris **l'iris**
(l)ee-rees

iron **(le) fer à repasser**
(luh) fayr ah ruh-pah-say

island **l'île**
(l)eel

jacket

(la) veste
(lah) vayst

jam

(la) confiture
(lah) kohn-fee-ture

jigsaw puzzle

(le) puzzle
(luh) poe-zl

jockey

(le) jockey
(luh) joh-kay

juggler

(le) jongleur
(luh) john-gloer

(to) jump

sauter
soh-tay

kangaroo **(le) kangourou**
(luh) kon-goo-roo

key **(la) clé**
(lah) cleh

kitten **(le) chaton**
(luh) shah-tohn

knife **(le) couteau**
(luh) koo-toh

knight **(le) chevalier**
(luh) sheh-vahl-yay

(to) knit **tricoter**
tree-koh-tay

knot **(le) noeud**
(luh) noe

koala bear **(le) koala**
(luh) koh-ah-lah

ladder   **l'échelle**
(l)eh-shel

ladybug   **(la) coccinelle**
(lah) cohk-see-nel

lamb   **l'agneau**
(l)ahn-yoh

lamp   **(la) lampe**
(lah) lonp

(to) lap   **laper**
lah-pay

laughter   **(le) rire**
(luh) reer

lavender   **(la) lavande**
(lah) lah-vond

lawn mower   **(la) tondeuse à gazon**
(lah) ton-does ah-gah-zohn

leaf   **(la) feuille**
(lah) foi-ye

leg   **(la) jambe**
(lah) jonb

lemon   **(le) citron**
(luh) see-trohn

lettuce   **(la) laitue**
(lah) lay-tu

lightbulb **l'ampoule**
(l)on-pool

lighthouse **(le) phare**
(luh) fahr

lilac **(le) lilas**
(luh) lee-lah

lion **(le) lion**
(luh) lee-yohn

(to) listen **écouter**
eh-koo-tay

lobster **(le) homard**
(luh) oh-mahr

lock

(la) serrure
(lah) say-rure

lovebird

(la) perruche
(lah) pay-rush

luggage

(le) bagage
(luh) bah-gahj

lumberjack

(le) bûcheron
(luh) bu-shuh-rohn

lunch

(le) déjeuner
(luh) deh-joe-nay

lynx

(le) lynx
(luh) lanx

magazine   **(le) magazine**
(luh) mah-gah-zeen

magician   **(le) magicien**
(luh) mah-jees-yayn

magnet   **l'aimant**
(l)ay-mon

map   **(la) carte**
(lah) cahrt

maple leaf   **(la) feuille d'érable**
(lah) foi-ye deh-rah-bl

marketplace   **(le) marché**
(luh) mahr-sheh

mask   **(le) masque**
(luh) mahsk

messy

en désordre
on deh-zohr-dr

milkman

(le) livreur de lait
(luh) lee-vroer duh lay

mirror

(le) miroir
(luh) meer-wahr

mitten

(la) moufle
(lah) moo-fl

money

l'argent
(l)ahr-jon

monkey

(le) singe
(luh) sanj

moon

(la) lune
(lah) lun

mother   **(la) mère**
(lah) mayr

mountain   **(la) montagne**
(lah) mohn-tahn-ye

mouse   **(la) souris**
(lah) soo-ree

mouth   **(la) bouche**
(lah) boosh

mushroom   **(le) champignon**
(luh) shon-peen-yohn

music   **(la) musique**
(lah) mu-zeek

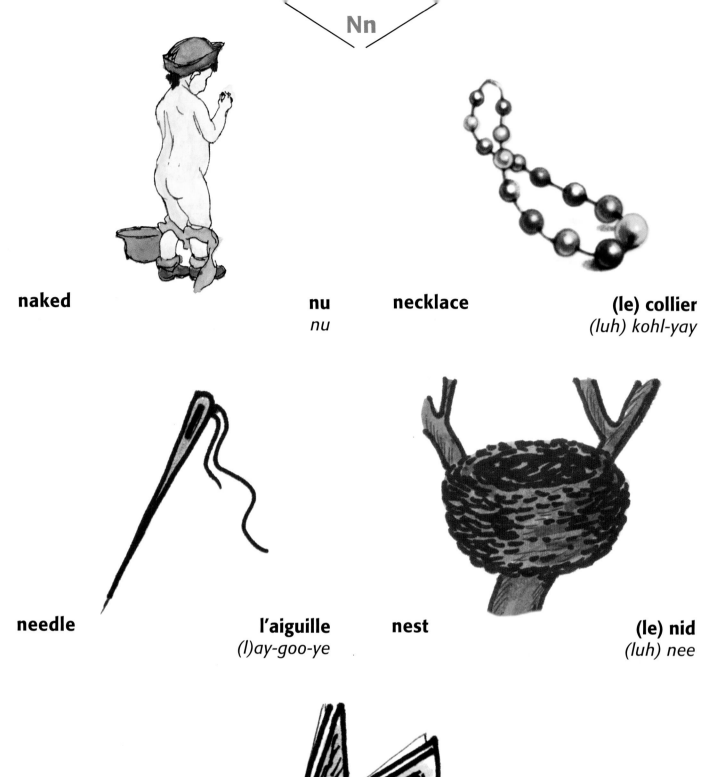

naked

nu
nu

necklace

(le) collier
(luh) kohl-yay

needle

l'aiguille
(l)ay-goo-ye

nest

(le) nid
(luh) nee

newspaper

(le) journal
(luh) joor-nahl

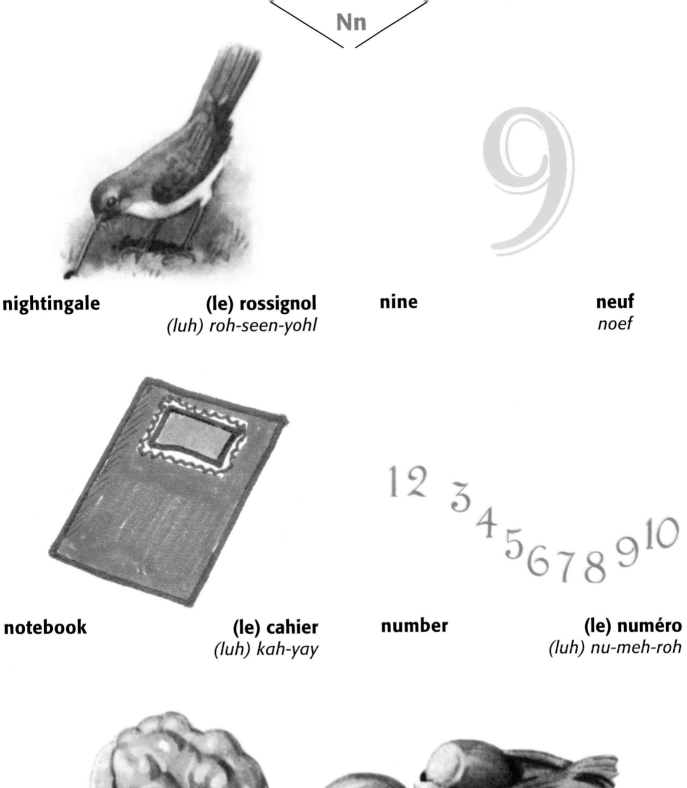

nightingale　　　　**(le) rossignol**
(luh) roh-seen-yohl

nine　　　　**neuf**
noef

notebook　　　　**(le) cahier**
(luh) kah-yay

number　　　　**(le) numéro**
(luh) nu-meh-roh

nut　　　　**(la) noix**
(lah) nwah

oar　　　　　　　　　**(la) rame**
(lah) rahm

ocean liner　　　　　**(le) paquebot**
(luh) pah-kuh-boh

old　　　　　　　　　**vieux**
vee-oe

one　　　　　　**un**　　　　**onion**　　　　　　**l'oignon**
ahn　　　　　　　　　　　　*(l)ohn-yohn*

open **ouvert**
oo-vayr

orange **l'orange**
(l)oh-ronj

ostrich **l'autruche**
(l)oh-trush

owl **(le) hibou**
(luh) ee-boo

ox **(le) boeuf**
(luh) boef

padlock **(le) cadenas**
(luh) ka-duh-nah

paint **(la) peinture**
(lah) payn-ture

painter **(le) peintre**
(luh) payn-tr

pajamas **(le) pyjama**
(luh) pee-jah-mah

palm tree **(le) palmier**
(luh) pahlm-yay

paper **(le) papier**
(luh) pahp-yay

parachute **(le) parachute**
(luh) pah-rah-shut

park (le) parc
(luh) pahrk

parrot (le) perroquet
(luh) pay-roh-keh

passport (le) passeport
(luh) pah-suh-pohr

patch (la) pièce
(lah) pee-es

path (le) chemin
(luh) shuh-man

peach (la) pêche
(lah) paysh

pear (la) poire
(lah) pwahr

pebble

(le) caillou
(luh) kah-you

(to) peck

becqueter
bay-kuh-tay

(to) peel

peler
puh-lay

pelican

(le) pélican
(luh) peh-lee-kon

pencil

(le) crayon
(luh) kray-yohn

penguin

(le) pingouin
(luh) pan-goo-an

people

(les) gens
(lay) john

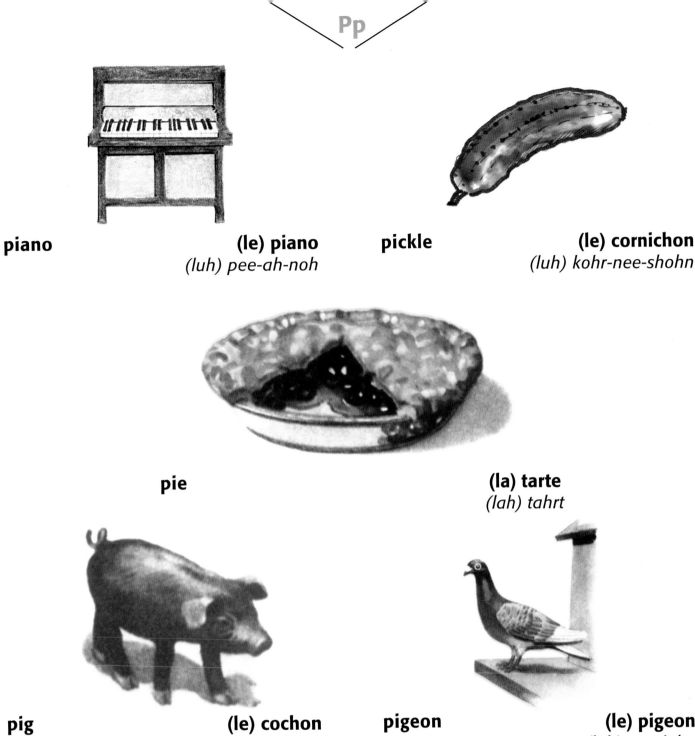

piano

(le) piano
(luh) pee-ah-noh

pickle

(le) cornichon
(luh) kohr-nee-shohn

pie

(la) tarte
(lah) tahrt

pig

(le) cochon
(luh) koh-shohn

pigeon

(le) pigeon
(luh) pee-john

pillow

l'oreiller
(l)oh-ray-yay

pin

l'épingle
(l)eh-pan-gl

pine　　　　　　**(le) pin**
(luh) pan

pineapple　　　　　**l'ananas**
(l)ah-nah-nah

pit　　　　　　**(le) noyau**
(luh) nwah-yoh

pitcher　　　　　**(la) cruche**
(lah) crewsh

plate　　　　　**l'assiette**
(l)ahs-yet

platypus　　　　**l'ornithorynque**
(l)ohr-nee-toh-rank

(to) play **jouer**
joo-ay

plum **(la) prune**
(lah) prun

polar bear **l'ours blanc**
(l)oors blon

pony **(le) poney**
(luh) poh-nay

pot **(le) pot**
(luh) poh

potato **(la) pomme de terre**
(lah) pohm duh tayr

(to) pour   **verser**
vayr-say

present   **(le) cadeau**
(luh) kah-doh

(to) pull   **tirer**
tee-ray

pumpkin   **(la) citrouille**
(lah) see-troo-ye

Qq

puppy   **(le) chiot**
(luh) shee-oh

queen   **(la) reine**
(lah) rayn

rabbit

(le) lapin
(luh) lah-pan

raccoon

(le) raton laveur
(luh) rah-tohn lah-voer

racket

(la) raquette
(lah) rah-ket

radio

(la) radio
(lah) rahd-yoh

radish

(le) radis
(luh) rah-dee

raft   **(le) radeau**   **rain**   **(la) pluie**
(luh) rah-doh   *(lah) ploo-ee*

rainbow   **l'arc-en-ciel**
(l)ahrk-ons-yayl

raincoat   **l'imperméable**   **raspberry**   **(la) framboise**
(l)an-payr-meh-ah-bl   *(la) fron-bwahs*

(to) read

lire
leer

red　　　　**rouge**
rooj

refrigerator　　**(le) réfrigérateur**
(luh) reh-free-jeh-rah-toer

rhinoceros　　　**(le) rhinocéros**
(luh) ree-noh-seh-rohs

ring　　　　**l'anneau**
(l)ah-noh

(to) ring

sonner
soh-nay

river

(le) fleuve
(luh) fluhv

road

(la) route
(lah) root

rocket

(la) fusée
(lah) fu-zeh

roof

(le) toit
(luh) twah

rooster

(le) coq
(luh) kohk

root   **(la) racine**
(lah) rah-seen

rope   **(la) corde**
(lah) kohrd

rose   **(la) rose**
(lah) rohz

(to) row   **ramer**
rah-may

ruler   **(la) règle**
(lah) ray-gl

(to) run   **courir**
koo-reer

safety pin   **l'épingle-de-nourrice**
(l)eh-pan-gl-duh-noo-rees

(to) sail   **naviguer**
nah-vee-gay

sailor   **(le) marin**
(luh) mah-ran

salt   **(le) sel**
(luh) sel

scarf   **l'écharpe**
(l)eh-sharp

school   **l'école**
(l)eh-kohl

scissors **(les) ciseaux**
(lay) see-zoh

screwdriver **(le) tournevis**
(luh) toor-nuh-vees

seagull **(la) mouette**
(lah) moo-et

seesaw **(la) bascule**
(lah) bahs-kul

seven **sept**
sayt

(to) sew **coudre**
koo-dr

shark   **(le) requin**
(luh) ruh-kan

sheep   **(le) mouton**
(luh) moo-tohn

shell   **(le) coquillage**
(luh) koh-kee-yahj

shepherd   **(le) berger**
(luh) bayr-jay

ship   **(le) navire**
(luh) nah-veer

shirt   **(la) chemise**
(lah) shuh-meez

shoe   **(la) chaussure**
(lah) shoh-sure

shovel   **(la) pelle**
(lah) pel

(to) show   **montrer**
mon-tray

shower   **(la) douche**
(lah) doosh

shutter   **(le) volet**
(luh) voh-leh

sick   **malade**
mah-lahd

sieve   **(le) tamis**
(luh) tah-mee

(to) sing   **chanter**
shon-tay

(to) sit   **être assis**
aytr ah-see

six   **six**
sees

sled   **(la) luge**
(lah) luj

(to) sleep   **dormir**
dohr-meer

small   **petit**
puh-tee

smile   **(le) sourire**
(luh) soo-reer

snail   **l'escargot**
(l)ays-kahr-goh

snake   **(le) serpent**
(luh) sayr-pon

snow   **(la) neige**
(lah) nayj

sock   **(la) chaussette**
(lah) shoh-set

sofa   **(le) sofa**
(luh) soh-fah

sparrow   **(le) moineau**
(luh) mwah-noh

spider   **l'araignée**
(l)ah-rayn-yeh

spiderweb   **(la) toile d'araignée**
(lah) twahl dah-rayn-yeh

spoon   **(la) cuillère**
(lah) kwee-yayr

squirrel   **l'écureuil**
(l)eh-ku-roi

stairs   **l'escalier**
(l)ays-kahl-yay

stamp   **(le) timbre**
(luh) tanbr

starfish   **l'étoile de mer**
(l)eh-twahl duh mayr

stork   **(la) cigogne**
(lah) see-gohn-ye

stove   **(le) fourneau**
(luh) foor-noh

strawberry   **(la) fraise**
(lah) frayz

subway   **(le) métro**
(luh) meh-troh

sugar cube   **(le) morceau de sucre**
(luh) mohr-so duh su-kr

sun   **(le) soleil**
(luh) so-lay

sunflower   **(le) tournesol**
(luh) toor-nuh-sohl

sweater   **(le) pullover**
(luh) pu-loh-vayr

(to) sweep   **balayer**
bah-lay-yay

swing   **(la) balançoire**
(lah) bah-lon-swahr

table **(la) table**
(lah) tah-bl

teapot **(la) théière**
(lah) teh-yayr

teddy bear **l'ours en peluche**
(l)oors on puh-lush

television **(la) télévision**
(lah) teh-leh-vees-yohn

10

ten **dix**
dees

tent **(la) tente**
(lah) tont

theater **(le) théâtre**
(luh) tay-ah-tr

thimble **(le) dé**
(luh) deh

(to) think **penser**
pon-say

three **trois**
trwah

tie **(la) cravate**
(lah) krah-vaht

(to) tie **lacer**
lah-say

tiger   **(le) tigre**
(luh) tee-gr

toaster   **(le) grille-pain**
(luh) gree-yuh-payn

tomato   **(la) tomate**
(lah) toh-maht

toucan   **le toucan**
(luh) too-kon

towel   **(la) serviette**
(lah) sayr-vee-yet

tower   **(la) tour**
(lah) toor

toy box   **(la) boîte à jouet**
(lah) bwaht ah joo-eh

tracks   **(les) voies**
(lay) vwah

train station   **(la) gare**
(lah) gahr

tray   **(le) plateau**
(luh) plah-toh

tree   **l'arbre**
(l)ahr-br

trough   **(la) mangeoire**
(lah) mon-jwahr

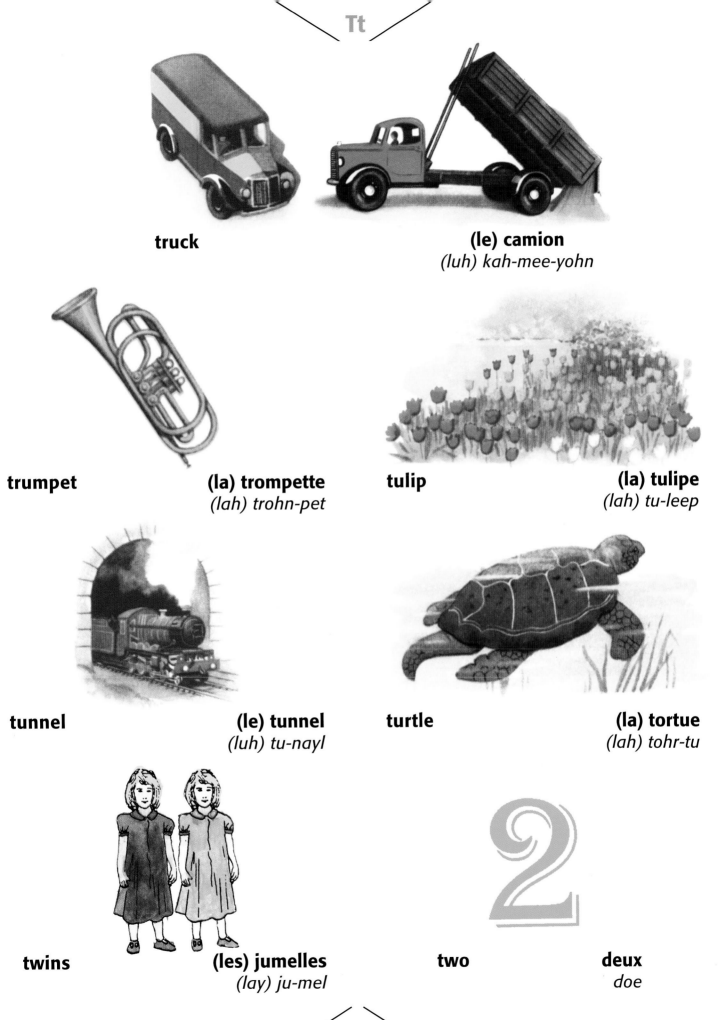

truck   **(le) camion**
(luh) kah-mee-yohn

trumpet   **(la) trompette**
(lah) trohn-pet

tulip   **(la) tulipe**
(lah) tu-leep

tunnel   **(le) tunnel**
(luh) tu-nayl

turtle   **(la) tortue**
(lah) tohr-tu

twins   **(les) jumelles**
(lay) ju-mel

two   **deux**
doe

umbrella **(le) parapluie** **uphill** **montant**
(luh) pah-rah-plu-ee *mohn-ton*

Vv

vase **(le) vase** **veil** **(le) voile**
(luh) vahz *(luh) vwahl*

village

(le) village
(luh) vee-lahj

violet

violet
(luh) vee-oh-leh

violin

(le) violon
(luh) vee-oh-lohn

voyage

(le) voyage
(luh) voh-yahj

waiter **(le) serveur**
(luh) sayr-voer

(to) wake up **se réveiller**
suh reh-vay-yay

walrus **(le) morse**
(luh) mohrs

(to) wash **laver**
lah-vay

watch **(la) montre**
(lah) mohn-tr

(to) watch **regarder**
ruh-gahr-day

(to) water   **arroser**
ah-roh-zay

waterfall   **(la) chute**
(lah) shute

watering can   **l'arrosoir**
(l)ah-roh-zwahr

watermelon   **(la) pastèque**
(lah) pahs-tayk

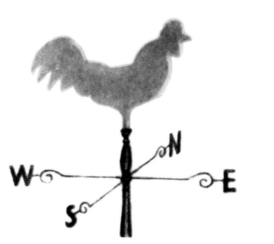

weather vane   **(la) girouette**
(lah) jee-roo-et

(to) weigh   **peser**
puh-zay

whale   **(la) baleine**
(lah) bah-layn

wheel   **(la) roue**
(lah) roo

wheelbarrow   **(la) brouette**
(lah) broo-et

whiskers   **(les) moustaches**
(lay) moos-tash

(to) whisper   **chuchoter**
shu-shoh-tay

whistle   **(le) siffl**
(luh) seef-fle

white   **blanc**
blon

wig   **(la) perruque**
(lah) pay-ruk

wind   **(le) vent**
(luh) von

window   **(la) fenêtre**
(lah) fuh-nay-tr

wings   **(les) ailes**
(lay) zayl

winter   **l'hivers**
(l)ee-vayr

wolf   **(le) loup**
                                          (luh) loo

wood   **(le) bois**   **word**   **(le) mot**
                    (luh) bwah   *(luh) moh*

(to) write   **écrire**
                                          eh-kreer

yellow

jaune
john

zebra

(le) zèbre
(luh) zeh-br

A

abeille (l')	bee
agneau (l')	lamb
aigle (l')	eagle
aiguille (l')	needle
ailes (les)	wings
aimant (l')	magnet
alligator (l')	alligator
alphabet (l')	alphabet
ami (l')	friend
ampoule (l')	lightbulb
ananas (l')	pineapple
âne (l')	donkey
anneau (l')	ring
antilope (l')	antelope
appareil de photo (l')	camera
aquarium (l')	aquarium
araignée (l')	spider
arbre de Noël (l')	Christmas tree
arbre (l')	tree
arc-en-ciel (l')	rainbow
argent (l')	money
arroser	(to) water
arrosoir (l')	watering can
assiette (l')	plate
Au revoir	"Good-bye"
aubergine (l')	eggplant
automne (l')	autumn
autoroute (l')	highway
autruche (l')	ostrich
avion (l')	airplane

B

bagage (le)	luggage
balai (le)	broom
balançoire (la)	swing
balayer	(to) sweep
baleine (la)	whale
balle (la)	ball
ballon (le)	balloon
banane (la)	banana

banc (le)	bench
bascule (la)	seesaw
bateau (le)	boat
bébé (le)	baby
becqueter	(to) peck
berceau (le)	cradle
berger (le)	shepherd
biche (la)	deer
bicyclette (la)	bicycle
biscuit (le)	cracker
blaireau (le)	badger
blanc	white
bleu	blue
blocs (les)	blocks
boeuf (le)	ox
boire	(to) drink
bois (les)	antlers
bois (le)	wood
boîte à jouet (la)	toy box
bol (le)	bowl
bonbon (le)	candy
Bonne nuit	"Good night"
botte (la)	boot
bouche (la)	mouth
bougie (la)	candle
boulanger (le)	baker
bourdon (le)	bumblebee
boussole (la)	compass
bouteille (la)	bottle
bracelet (le)	bracelet
branche (la)	branch
brosse (la)	brush
brouette (la)	wheelbarrow
bûcheron (le)	lumberjack
bureau (le)	desk

C

cactus (le)	cactus
cadeau (le)	present
cadenas (le)	padlock
cadre (le)	frame
café (le)	café
cage (la)	birdcage
cahier (le)	notebook
caillou (le)	pebble
camion (le)	truck

canard (le)	duck
canoë (le)	canoe
capitaine (le)	captain
carotte (la)	carrot
carrosse (le)	coach
carte (la)	card; map
casquette (la)	cap
castor (le)	beaver
ceinture (la)	belt
cerise (la)	cherry
chaise (la)	chair
chameau (le)	camel
champ (le)	field
champignon (le)	mushroom
chanter	(to) sing
chapeau (le)	hat
chat (le)	cat
château (le)	castle
chaton (le)	kitten
chaussette (la)	sock
chaussure (la)	shoe
chauve-souris (la)	bat
chemin (le)	path
cheminée (la)	chimney
chemise (la)	shirt
chercher	(to) gather
cheval (le)	horse
chevalier (le)	knight
chèvre (la)	goat
chien (le)	dog
chiot (le)	puppy
chocolat (le)	chocolate
chou (le)	cabbage
chuchoter	(to) whisper
chute (la)	waterfall
cigogne (la)	stork
cinq	five
cirque (le)	circus
ciseaux (les)	scissors
citron (le)	lemon
citrouille (la)	pumpkin
clé (la)	key

J

jambe (la)	leg
jardin (le)	garden
jaune	yellow
jockey (le)	jockey
jongleur (le)	juggler
jouer	(to) play
journal (le)	newspaper
jumelles (les)	binoculars; twins

K

kangourou (le)	kangaroo
koala (le)	koala bear

L

lacer	(to) tie
laitue (la)	lettuce
lampe (la)	lamp
laper	(to) lap
lapin (le)	rabbit
lavande (la)	lavender
laver	(to) wash
libellule (la)	dragonfly
liège (le)	cork
lilas (le)	lilac
lion (le)	lion
lire	(to) read
lit (le)	bed
livre (le)	book
livreur de lait (le)	milkman
locomotive (la)	engine
loup (le)	wolf
luge (la)	sled
lune (la)	moon
lunettes (les)	glasses
lynx (le)	lynx

M

magazine (le)	magazine
magicien (le)	magician
main (la)	hand
maïs (le)	corn
maison (la)	house
maison de poupée (la)	dollhouse
malade	sick
mangeoire (la)	trough
manger	(to) eat
manteau (le)	coat
marché (le)	marketplace
marcher à quatre pattes	(to) crawl
marin (le)	sailor
marron	brown
marteau (le)	hammer
masque (le)	mask
mère (la)	mother
métro (le)	subway
meuble (le)	furniture
miel (le)	honey
miroir (le)	mirror
moineau (le)	sparrow
moisson (la)	harvest
montagne (la)	mountain
montant	uphill
montre (la)	watch
montrer	(to) show
morceau de sucre (le)	sugar cube
morse (le)	walrus
mot (le)	word
mouchoir (le)	handkerchief
mouette (la)	seagull
moufle (la)	mitten
moustaches (les)	whiskers
mouton (le)	sheep
musique (la)	music

N

naviguer	(to) sail
navire (le)	ship
neige (la)	snow
neuf	nine
niche (la)	doghouse
nid (le)	nest
noeud (le)	knot
noir	black
noix (la)	nut
noix de coco (la)	coconut
nourrir	(to) feed
noyau (le)	pit
nu	naked
nuage (le)	cloud
numéro (le)	number

O

oeil (l')	eye
oeuf (l')	egg
oie (l')	goose
oignon (l')	onion
oiseau (l')	bird
orange (l')	orange
oreiller (l')	pillow
orge (l')	barley
ornithorynque (l')	platypus
os (l')	bone
ours (l')	bear
ours blanc (l')	polar bear
ours en peluche (l')	teddybear
ouvert	open

P

pain (le)	bread
palmier (le)	palm tree
panache (le)	headdress
panier (le)	basket
papier (le)	paper
papillon (le)	butterfly
paquebot (le)	ocean liner
parachute (le)	parachute
parapluie (le)	umbrella
parc (le)	park
passeport (le)	passport
pastèque (la)	watermelon

Folk Tales from Bohemia

Adolf Wenig

This folk tale collection is one of a kind, focusing uniquely on humankind's struggle with evil in the world. Delicately ornate red and black text and illustrations set the mood.

Ages 9 and up

90 pages • red and black illustrations • 5 1/2 x 8 1/4 • 0-7818-0718-2 • W • $14.95hc • (786)

Czech, Moravian and Slovak Fairy Tales

Parker Fillmore

Fifteen different classic, regional folk tales and 23 charming illustrations whisk the reader to places of romance, deception, royalty, and magic.

Ages 12 and up

243 pages • 23 b/w illustrations • 5 1/2 x 8 1/4 • 0-7818-0714-X • W • $14.95 hc • (792)

Glass Mountain: Twenty-Eight Ancient Polish Folk Tales and Fables

W.S. Kuniczak

Illustrated by Pat Bargielski

As a child in a far-away misty corner of Volhynia, W.S. Kuniczak was carried away to an extraordinary world of magic and illusion by the folk tales of his Polish nurse.

171 pages • 6 x 9 • 8 illustrations • 0-7818-0552-X • W • $16.95hc • (645)

Old Polish Legends

Retold by F.C. Anstruther

Wood engravings by J. Sekalski

This fine collection of eleven fairy tales, with an introduction by Zymunt Nowakowski, was first published in Scotland during World War II.

66 pages • 7 1/4 x 9 • 11 woodcut engravings • 0-7818-0521-X • W • $11.95hc • (653)

Folk Tales from Russia

by Donald A. Mackenzie

With nearly 200 pages and 8 full-page black-and-white illustrations, the reader will be charmed by these legendary folk tales that symbolically weave magical fantasy with the historic events of Russia's past.

Ages 12 and up

192 pages • 8 b/w illustrations • 5 1/2 x 8 1/4 • 0-7818-0696-8 • W • $12.50hc • (788)

Fairy Gold: A Book of Classic English Fairy Tales

Chosen by Ernest Rhys

Illustrated by Herbert Cole

Forty-nine imaginative black and white illustrations accompany thirty classic tales, including such beloved stories as "Jack and the Bean Stalk" and "The Three Bears."

Ages 12 and up

236 pages • 5 1/2 x 8 1/4 • 49 b/w illustrations • 0-7818-0700-X • W • $14.95hc • (790)

Tales of Languedoc: From the South of France

Samuel Jacques Brun

For readers of all ages, here is a masterful collection of folk tales from the south of France.

Ages 12 and up

248 pages • 33 b/w sketches • 5 1/2 x 8 1/4 • 0-7818-0715-8 • W • $14.95hc • (793)

Twenty Scottish Tales and Legends

Edited by Cyril Swinson

Illustrated by Allan Stewart

Twenty enchanting stories take the reader to an extraordinary world of magic harps, angry giants, mysterious spells and gallant Knights.

Ages 9 and up

215 pages • 5 1/2 x 8 1/4 • 8 b/w illustrations • 0-7818-0701-8 • W • $14.95 hc • (789)

Swedish Fairy Tales

Translated by H. L. Braekstad

A unique blending of enchantment, adventure, comedy, and romance make this collection of Swedish fairy tales a must-have for any library.

Ages 9 and up

190 pages • 21 b/w illustrations • 51/2 x 81/4 • 0-7818-0717-4 • W • $12.50hc • (787)

The Little Mermaid and Other Tales

Hans Christian Andersen

Here is a near replica of the first American edition of 27 classic fairy tales from the masterful Hans Christian Andersen.

Ages 9 and up

508 pages • b/w illustrations • 6 x 9 • 0-7818-0720-4 • W • $19.95hc • (791)

Pakistani Folk Tales: Toontoony Pie and Other Stories

Ashraf Siddiqui and Marilyn Lerch

Illustrated by Jan Fairservis

In these 22 folk tales are found not only the familiar figures of folklore—kings and beautiful princesses—but the magic of the Far East, cunning jackals, and wise holy men.

Ages 7 and up

158 pages • 6 1/2 x 8 1/2 • 38 illustrations • 0-7818-0703-4 • W • $12.50hc • (784)

Folk Tales from Chile

Brenda Hughes

This selection of 15 tales gives a taste of the variety of Chile's rich folklore. Fifteen charming illustrations accompany the text.

Ages 7 and up

121 pages • 5 1/2 x 8 1/4 • 15 illustrations • 0-7818-0712-3 • W • $12.50hc • (785)

All prices subject to change. **To purchase Hippocrene Books** contact your local bookstore, call (718) 454-2366, or write to: HIPPOCRENE BOOKS, 171 Madison Avenue, New York, NY 10016. Please enclose check or money order, adding $5.00 shipping (UPS) for the first book and $.50 for each additional book.